Million Dollar MLM
Shortcut

Jay Noland

LEGAL NOTICE

The Publisher has strived to be as accurate and complete as possible in the creation of this report, notwithstanding the fact that he does not warrant or represent at any time that the contents within are accurate due to the rapidly changing nature of the Internet.

While all attempts have been made to verify information provided in this publication, the Publisher assumes no responsibility for errors, omissions, or contrary interpretation of the subject matter herein. Any perceived slights of specific persons, peoples, or organizations are unintentional.

In practical advice books, like anything else in life, there are no guarantees of income made. Readers are cautioned to rely on their own judgment about their individual circumstances to act accordingly.

This book is not intended for use as a source of legal, business, accounting or financial advice. All readers are advised to seek services of competent professionals in the legal, business, accounting, and finance fields.

Library of Congress Control Number:		2015955703
ISBN-13:	Paperback:	978-1-68256-158-4
	PDF:	978-1-68256-159-1
	ePub:	978-1-68256-160-7
	Kindle:	978-1-68256-161-4

Printed in the United States of America

LitFire LLC
1-800-511-9787
www.litfirepublishing.com
order@litfirepublishing.com

Enforcement of Copyright

Jay Noland MLM (Enhanced Capital Funding) takes the protection of its copyright very seriously.

If it is discovered that you have used its copyright materials in contravention of the license above, we will bring legal proceedings against you seeking monetary damages and an injunction to stop you from using those materials. You could also be ordered to pay legal costs.

If you become aware of any use of these copyright materials that contravenes or may contravene the license above, please report this by email to sales@jaynolandmlm.com

Million Dollar MLM Shortcut

"Learn the Immediate Million Dollar <u>Shortcuts</u> to Take Your MLM Business to <u>Incredible</u> Heights as Practiced by MILLIONAIRE Networkers from Around the World!"

Table of Contents

INTRODUCTION

This book is about providing a simplified "Shortcut" to building a "Multi-Million Dollar" MLM Business. You will find the philosophies in this book to be straightforward and to the point. My career thus far in MLM has been nothing short of amazing. Through the experiences and knowledge I've gained, I've been fortunate enough to have built sales organizations in excess of 500,000 Distributors in my nearly 2 decades of being involved in the MLM Industry. My Sales Organizations at the time of the printing of this book have produced approximately a Billion Dollars in sales. My trainings have now produced some of the Top Active Money Earners in the entire MLM Industry. I've found that creating Millionaires through MLM is simple when you have students who are hungry, eager, and committed to learn how to become successful in this industry.

Through this book you will get to bypass the trial and error, and the Millions of Dollars it cost me to learn what I've learned.

This book will also smash any "myths" about building a Multi-Million Dollar MLM Business. For example, there's a "myth" that says you have to be "Born" with "Super Talent" to become a Million Dollar Earner in MLM. Another common myth is that you have to "Lucky" in order to become a Million Dollar Earner in MLM. Both of these "myths" couldn't be farther from the truth. Million Dollar Earners in MLM are not born with "Super Talent," they build themselves to become a "Super Talent." Million Dollar Earners in MLM are not "Lucky." They work hard and develop the skills to become what people call "Lucky." This book will give you the skills to dispel these "myths," as well as any others that would have you to believe you can't become a tremendous success in this industry.

Why waste time and take the long route trying to figure out what it takes to build a Multi-Million Dollar MLM Business when you have a Shortcut?

My mission with this book is to provide you the "Shortcut" to building a Multi-Million Dollar MLM Business. I want to see people Financially Free, and that includes you. The MLM Industry has done so much for myself and family. Now it's time for me to give back to the entire industry. This book is one in the many ways that I look to give back. I'm making it extremely affordable for anyone who wants to learn how to build a Multi-Million Dollar MLM Business to be able to do so.

If you've got the desire, hunger, and are teachable, I truly believe this book will set you on a course that many have only dreamed about.

I believe in you, and now it's time for you to believe in yourself more than you ever have before. Most people only need some direction, and I promise through this book to provide that direction to you. Now, it's time for you to stop standing in line. It's time for you to take advantage of the "Million Dollar MLM Shortcut."

Chapter 1

Take Off: Get Your Success Out The Ground

1.1 The Airplane And The Rocket Ship

If you've ever been on an airplane before then you know it takes an incredible amount of energy and speed to get the plane off the ground. It actually takes a plane (like a B-757) about 160–180 MPH to get off the ground. You need to think of your MLM Business in the same way. Put all your energy and effort to create speed so your business can actually get off the ground. There are some runways that even have the ocean at the end of it. If the plane doesn't lift off, the plane will go right into the ocean. Just as focused as the pilot is to make sure that plane lifts off and doesn't fall into the ocean, is just as focused as you need to be to get your MLM Business off the ground.

Take a Rocket Ship for example. Approximately 90% of the entire fuel for the mission is used just in the lift off. The rest of the mission is run on the remaining 10%. Focus your MLM Business in the same manner as the Rocket Ship taking off from the launching pad. If you want to be a Million Dollar MLM Producer and Earner, then you have to put your initial energy into your business to get it off the "launching pad" just like the Rocket Ship. If you do it right, you'll be able to run the rest of your career on the remaining 10%. Just imagine, a Lifetime of Incredible Residual Income, because you properly launched your MLM Business off the ground.

1.2 The Right Mindset From The Beginning

It's important to have the right mindset from the beginning. Million Dollar Earners in MLM treat their MLM Business like a BUSINESS from the very beginning. They make a quick distinction in their minds from the beginning and put the proper value on their MLM Business.

There are 3 different types of businesses to distinguish from:

1. Traditional Business
2. Franchise Business
3. MLM/Network Marketing Business

Traditional Business

A "Traditional Business" typically takes a large amount of capital to start up. For example, to open a typical restaurant will usually range from $250,000 and up. Then you have to deal with all the "headaches" like employees, worker's comp, payroll tax, supplies, inventory, insurance, accounting, advertising, office rent/building costs, permits, payment systems/merchant accounts, and more. And with all these "headaches" a person has to deal with, they still have a 85% chance they'll fail in their very first year. For most people, they don't have the large capital required to start, they don't want to deal with the "headaches," and they don't want to take an 85% risk that they'll fail and lose everything.

Franchise Business

A great "Franchise Business" model has a "Success System" in place. That system allows the head Franchise Owner to charge a hefty Franchise Fee to those who want to own one of their franchises. For example, the most successful franchise system in the world is McDonald's. They don't have the best hamburgers, but they sell the most because of their system. The thing is, their system (franchise) will cost you approximately $1.5 Million! Then you still typically have to wait 3-5 years to even see a profit. Most people don't have an extra $1.5 Million laying around, so buying a successful Franchise Business is not an option for most people.

MLM/Network Marketing Business

This leaves the last option, which now the masses are starting to pay attention to... the MLM/Network Marketing Business. A MLM Business is so attractive because the start up costs are very low (typically $500 - $1,500) to get started, but the Profit Potential is extremely high. With an MLM/Network Marketing Business you don't have all the "headaches" to deal with either. You don't have employees, worker's comp, payroll tax, large inventory, product research, packaging, design, manufacturing, insurance, heavy accounting, office rent/ building costs, permits, payment systems/merchant accounts, etc. With a MLM/Network Marketing Business you primarily have to focus on marketing your products and recruiting others to do the same.

Because it is so "inexpensive" to get involved with an MLM/ Network Marketing Business, and because you don't have to deal with all the "headaches," most people simply don't take the business seriously and thus fail. Million Dollar MLM Earners are different than most everyone else, because they consciously distinguish the fact that they have to treat their MLM/Network Marketing Business just as if they put up the hundreds of thousands or millions of dollars it would take to start a Traditional Business or a Franchise Business. For example, in the minds of Million Dollar MLM Earners, they treat the $500 or so they put up to get started as if they put up $500,000. If a person has to put up that kind of money, they will take their business seriously. Having the ability to "mentally" trick your brain with this mindset is what separates Million Dollar Earners in the MLM Industry from everyone else.

If you're going to build a Multi-Million Dollar MLM Business, then you've got to make sure to treat it like a Multi-Million

Dollar Business. The MLM/Network Marketing Business will pay you the way you treat it.

1.3 Don't Be Average

Average means being "typical, common, or ordinary." Being average will never help you become a Million Dollar Earner in the MLM Industry. You have to focus on becoming EXCELLENT! This means you have to become outstanding, remarkable, superior, and extraordinary. Don't concentrate on small targets and small goals. Set your bar extremely high. You may have heard the saying "Shoot for the moon, and if you miss at least you'll hit the stars!" I agree with this philosophy full heartedly. Anyone can be average. It takes minimum effort to be average. Minimum effort equals minimum money. Big money takes Big Effort.

In order to be excellent and avoid being "average," you have to put the power of leverage to work for you immediately. You have to utilize the efforts of other people. Average distributors typically focus on trying to do everything themselves... calling, presenting, selling, and then trying to do all 3 (calling, presenting, and selling) for their team too. NOOOO! Don't do this. This does not provide you any leverage.

Of course you need to make calls, do presentations, and sell your product. Of course you need to "help" your new prospects and team do the same, but your method of help needs to be focused on getting them to do it even when you are not around. They need to duplicate this with their teams as well. Focus on developing a large group of people who can duplicate simple steps like calling, presenting, and selling. This will keep you from being average. Duplicating is what makes you a Star in this industry.

1.4 IPA's

IPA's stands for "Income Producing Activities." To launch or re-launch your MLM Business you need to get your business off the ground by immediately focusing on "Income Producing Activities." Don't get caught in the trap of being busy without results. You need to duplicate this with your team as well.

I've taught for years the philosophy of "Activity versus Productivity." 95% or more new and existing Network Marketers fool themselves into thinking that just because they're "Active" that they are being productive. This comes from the "Job Mentality" where you just have to show up and be busy and still get a paycheck. I've seen it time and time again, where distributors get started and become extremely "busy" and expect a "paycheck" to come in. It doesn't work this way in MLM... it's not happening. You've got to focus on results, and IPA's are what bring results.

Let's break this down a little further...

Here are some "Activities" that trap people into thinking they're doing what they should be doing:

1. Constantly preparing and not doing.
2. Attending presentations by themselves.
3. Posting on Social Networks hoping that someone will recruit themselves.
4. Spending tons of time talking to their upline and sidelines (people already in the business, not in their organization).
5. Constantly studying and not applying.

Avoid spending too much time doing any of the above if you hope to have any major success in MLM/Network Marketing.

MLM is a contact business. You've got to contact people and build relationships. You've got to contact people and sell product. You've got to contact people and sponsor them in the business.

Most of the time people do these types of Non-IPA "Activities" to avoid actually having to do what it takes to be successful, which is contacting and persuading people to either buy their product or join their business.

You have to focus on IPA's (Income Producing Activities) such as:

1. Personally selling your product.
2. Personally prospecting and setting appointments (1 on 1's and Group Presentations).
3. Personally presenting your opportunity to a minimum of 4 people per day (1 on 1's or Group Presentations) at least 5 days per week.
4. Following up with potential Retail Customers.
5. Following up with Prospects to set more appointments
6. Training your new team members how to do the above (1 or 2 times per week. Maximum 2 hours training, then get back after it).

The Million Dollar MLM Earners focus on doing the IPA's I've just covered on a daily basis without fail. No matter how "busy" their day can get or how many "distractions" try to get in the way, Million Dollar MLM Earners push through and make sure they get IPA's done on a daily basis.

The best way to get this done is by breaking down your time. This is simple. Spend 80% of your time on IPA's and 20% of your time doing other things like planning organizing, studying, etc. This means that if you work your MLM Business an average of 4 hours per day, you will spend approximately 3 hours and 15 minutes on IPA's and about 45 minutes on Non-IPA's.

Remember to duplicate this focus with your team, so that you have the power of "leverage" working for you. To start, recruit 10 new people who commit to maximizing IPA's 5 to 6 days per week. If you do this, you have the potential to have your business explode!

Chapter 2

Maximize The Law Of Averages

2.1 The Numbers Tell The Whole Story

Million Dollar MLM Earners typically get off to a Fast Start. This is not always the case, but it is true in most cases. If you had the choice of becoming a Million Dollar MLM Producer Fast or Slow, which would you choose? I'm sure you answered... FAST!

To get off to a Fast Start, it is important that you learn to maximize the "Law of Averages" by going through the "numbers." You'll find that the "numbers" will tell you everything about yourself and about your team. No matter what your level of expertise, if you present your opportunity with excitement and passion, you will eventually sponsor someone. What's important to understand is that what you may lack in talent you can make up for in sheer effort (numbers). If you are willing to talk to enough people with the focus on becoming good at "closing," then it is only a matter of time before you get good at it.

This book however is focused on getting you off to a Million Dollar MLM "Fast Start" by giving you the "Shortcut" to MLM Success. This means that you have to be willing to learn and apply quicker than most. Remember this... Don't Settle. You can be as good as you want to be, but you can't settle for being anything less than your best. The "numbers" will help you quickly find out what you are good at and what you need to work on. The "numbers" will also be a great "feedback monitor" to tell what type of talent that you have on your team. It is important that you get your team to follow suit and duplicate the philosophy of the "Law of Averages." You have to fully buy into the fact that the "Numbers Tell The Whole Story."

To get off to a Million Dollar MLM "Fast Start," I recommend that you personally attempt to recruit 100 people as fast as possible. By doing so, you will begin to see a <u>Ratio</u>. It shouldn't take you that long to attempt to recruit 100 people if you are focused on IPA's (Income Producing Activities) as we spoke of in the prior chapter. If you are focused on recruiting at least 4 people per day, then it will only take you 25 days or less to attempt to recruit 100 people. Notice I use the word "attempt," because you're not going to sign up everyone of the 100 people. However, you should sign up some of the people. This will give you the <u>ratio</u> I'm speaking about. If you sign up 5 out of the 100 you attempt to recruit, your ratio would be 1:20. This means you are averaging sponsoring 1 person for every 20 people you attempt recruit.

Once you have a Ratio, you will start to have the "Law of Averages" work in your favor. You will start to see a trend. So as you can see, the "numbers" are telling you the "story" of how good you are. In order to start getting what is considered "good" at MLM, you need to start hitting a 1:10 Ratio. This means for every 10 people you show the business to, you should sponsor at least 1. Once you start hitting a 2:10 Ratio, you will be considered Above Average. You should start to see some nice checks starting to roll in at this point. Then once you start closing at a 3:10 Ratio, you have the opportunity to make Millions of Dollars. Think of Professional Baseball as an example. Players that can get "base hits" successfully 3 out of 10 times in Baseball are paid Millions of Dollars. This means they are failing 7 out of 10 times. However, it doesn't matter that they are failing more. What matters is they are hitting safely 3 out of 10 times, and for that, they are paid Millions of Dollars.

MLM/Network Marketing works in the same way. It doesn't matter how much you fail as long as you get to an Above Average Ratio (2:10 or better). By the way, the best of the best (Million Dollar Income Earners) typically can only get a 4:10 Ratio. This still means they are failing more than winning at recruiting, yet they earn Millions.

The "numbers" come down to this: The more the "quantity," the more the "quality," the higher your "closing ratio." Focus on turning up your "numbers" and you'll notice that you'll begin to get better and better. Use this same philosophy to teach your team. The numbers will tell you where you stand at all times. The numbers will also be a measuring stick of where your team stands at all times. Remember that increasing your "numbers" (quantity) will help you maximize the "Law of Averages."

2.2 Remove Emotion, Replace With Passion

Another important skill to develop is learning to "Remove Emotion, and Replace with Passion." To become great at the "Law of Averages" in the MLM/Network Marketing Industry and increase your "Ratio," you have to learn to not take things personally when someone doesn't get started in your business or buy your products. You have to set your mind on the fact that "most" people are not going to do this business. You don't need everyone to do this business. Always remember the analogy we spoke of before about "baseball" (3 out of 10 equals Millions of Dollars).

Removing the "emotion" (not taking things personal) out of your MLM Business will make your road to success much faster. Instead of taking things personally when someone doesn't join your business or purchase your products, focus on the fact that you don't need everyone to join. You just need to hit your ratio. A successful business owner understands right away that not everyone is going to buy from them. They understand that they only need a "percentage" of people to buy from them (ratio).

Successful Million Dollar Earners in the MLM/Network

Marketing Industry replace "emotion" with "PASSION." They become passionate about presenting their products and business opportunity to as many people as possible, knowing that a percentage of people will buy from them and join them. They know the "Law of Averages" works, period.

It's very important for you to get off to a fast start so you can pump even more "PASSION" into your business. Learn to replace the emotion with passion, and you'll be well on your way to maximizing the "Law of Averages.

2.3 Increase Your Skills

Another way to maximize the "Law of Averages" and better your closing "ratio" is increasing your skills. The better your skills, the better your ratio, period. How does someone go from a 1:10 Ratio to a 3:10 Ratio, or even better yet a 4:10 Ratio? They develop stronger skills.

How do you increase your skills?

This is where the previous chapter 2.1 comes in (The Numbers Tell The Whole Story). The more you practice, the better you get. Most people simply don't give themselves enough practice to become great at the MLM Business. You, however, are reading this book, because you are committed to taking advantage of the "Shortcut" to MLM Success. This means you're willing to do whatever it takes to be successful. Being successful means you have to develop sharper skills. So, it's time to practice. As soon as you're done reading this book, start practicing your presentation for your MLM Business on 100 Prospects. The great thing about "practicing" on Prospects is that some of them will sign up in your business. You'll be earning while you're learning! From that point, you will get a true gauge on where you are and what you have to do.

I promise you that if you apply what you've already learned in the previous chapters, you will start to see your skills increase. Once your skills increase, you will get direct feedback in the form of closing more sales (Retail and Sponsorships).

2.4 Track Your Progress (Critical)

I cannot stress enough the importance of tracking your progress. This allows you to remove the guess work out of your business. Again, remember the teaching in Chapter 2.1 (The Numbers Tell The Whole Story)? Well, you have to "TRACK" those "NUMBERS." You will not be able to know what your "RATIO" is unless you track your numbers. This is another one of the major causes of failure in the MLM/Network Marketing Industry. Most simply don't "track their numbers."

Tracking your progress brings professionalism to your business. It also brings a level of what I call "success expectancy" to your business. When you track your progress and start to see your ratio, then you know that with every certain number of people you talk to, you are either sponsoring or selling product to a certain amount of people.

I remember when I first started in the MLM Industry back in 1995. My upline and mentors were adamant about their team tracking their progress. When I started doing so, I realized I was sponsoring about 1 in every 8 people I showed the opportunity to. This raised my "success expectancy," which kept me going while I was growing.

Remember those first 100 Prospects I talked about in the previous chapter? This is the time that you now apply this skill.

You need to track each and every person you personally show your business opportunity to. Watch closely to see what your ratio is after every 10 people you show your plan to.

Professionalize your business from the beginning and "TRACK Your Progress." You'll more than likely notice that by you applying this technique (skill), you will start outperforming many others in your company.

Get ready to be amazed.

2.5 Great Habits Equals Great Success

Taking advantage of the "Law of Averages" comes down to developing and maintaining Great Habits! Start your MLM Business off the right way utilizing the "Shortcut" techniques in this book. This is vitally important, because if you develop bad habits, they're hard to break. On the other hand, if you develop great habits, you will be able to enjoy success much quicker and for the long term.

Make everything you learned thus far and the rest of the teachings of this book a habit. This will only help you to make more money faster.

The more you make it a habit of helping others quickly get their business off the ground, keeping the right mindset (treating your MLM business like a business), not settling for average results, focusing on income producing activities (IPA's), working the numbers, staying passionate and not emotional, increasing your skills, tracking your progress, along with the rest of the skills you'll learn in this book, the more you'll have the opportunity to truly build a Multi-Million Dollar MLM Business.

The definition of the word habit is "acquired behavior pattern regularly followed until it has become almost involuntary." Imagine having the ability to make millions of dollars almost "involuntary." That's what happens when you pick up the habits of the Million Dollar Earners in the MLM/Network Marketing Industry. The "Million Dollar MLM Shortcut" philosophy presented in this book can help you pick up these great habits, and great habits equals great money.

2.6 Be Relentless

Persistence beats Resistance EVERY TIME. To build a Multi-Million Dollar MLM Business you have to be persistent. A better word to relate the importance of this is RELENTLESS. You have to literally be relentless when it comes to taking the "Shortcut" to success. When I talked about getting your business off the ground in the first chapter, I mentioned the analogy of the Rocket Ship. I want you to imagine the fire and heat that's coming out of those engines to get the Rocket Ship off the launching pad. That heat represents the relentless focus that Million Dollar MLM Earners have when it comes to <u>making</u> their business a success.

To maximize the "Law of Averages," you are going to have to be relentless. Make up your mind now that no one is going to stop you. Keep bringing the "heat" and the "push" until you have the Multi-Million Dollar MLM Business that you are desiring.

Being relentless is a decision between you and you. No one can do it for you. As a matter of fact, no one will do it for you. You're going to have to take it. Don't let it happen. Make it happen. That's what being "relentless" is all about.

Chapter 3

Traditional Income Vs. Residual Income

3.1 Breaking Traditions

The Million Dollar MLM Shortcut is about breaking away from being average, and this means you're going to have to break old traditions that don't work. When it comes to making money, most people turn to a job. Why is this? This is because most people have been trained by our governments and school systems to become an "employee," and this means you have a job. The strange thing about this is that almost every person knows that working a job does not provide Financial Freedom. As a matter of a fact, a job for the most part leads to Financial Ruin... a life filled with debt and frustration.

It's understandable for the most part because most people don't know there are better options for making money available to them. This is where you come in. You have to show as many people as possible the MLM Industry to give them a way out. However, you have to start with yourself first.

To build a Multi-Million Dollar MLM Business, you have to tear away from the traditional process of making money immediately. Not only do you have to tear away from this method of making money, you have to lead others away from this "way of life" as well.

I'm not telling anyone to immediately quit their job. But I am telling everyone to immediately start building their MLM/ Network Marketing Business quickly enough to get their business off the ground and producing profits in order to have the opportunity to be free. Traditional methods of making money leaves you next to no chance to be free.

When I first saw the industry back in 1995, I immediately quit my job and have never had to go back to a job ever since. I've also seen other people immediately quit their jobs and then have to go back to a job. Why does this happen? Why does a person have to go back to a job? They have to go back to a job, because they didn't immediately focus on the principles that are being taught in this book. Most companies don't put all these things I'm teaching you in this book into one place where their distributors can easily find it. Why is this? I don't know. But what I do know is that I've been teaching distributors these principles for years and have seen a tremendous amount of success.

When I've worked with my teams, I immediately started to teach them these principles and the results have been staggering!

Again, I'm not telling anyone to immediately quit their job as I did. Most people can't handle it, because they're not properly trained and prepared. What I typically teach is that if you have a job, keep it until you match your income at least 6 months in a row. From there, you can make your own decisions. Do what feels right in your heart to do. The key is to not stay at a job too long, because it typically crushes your chances at achieving Financial Independence.

Breaking Traditions is something you have to embrace. You're more than likely going to be considered a "rebel" when you break traditions, but if you apply these principles you'll be a rebel with a big bank account.

3.2 Traditional Income

Traditional Income is trading your hours for pay. The technical term for this is called "Linear Income." Linear income means you only get paid when you work. Wealthy people will tell you that if this your method for making money, you are nuts.

Most think that just working a "job" is the only way people

make Linear Income. The fact is, nearly everyone that is "self-employed" is also working on Linear Income. Good examples of this are Doctors, Lawyers, Accountants, Plumbers, Electricians, etc. All are mostly exchanging their hours for pay. If they don't go to work, they don't get paid. It's nearly impossible to become Financially Independent this way. There are some who "invest" their money and eventually achieve Financial Success, but investing is another way of making income separate from what they are doing. Many people are never able to accumulate enough money to "invest" and thus stay stuck in a Liner Income position for life.

There are only so many hours in a day, and with Linear Income you can only be at one place at one time. <u>Having</u> to be there to make money doesn't allow you to have any leverage, and leverage is what allows you to duplicate your efforts and your money. 98% of the population are stuck in a Linear Income career and eventually fail miserably when it comes to finances. 2% of the population recognize what I call the "Linear Income Trap" and focus on making Residual Income so they can be free (more on this in the next chapter).

If you want freedom, then you need to start breaking away from Traditional Income (Linear Income). MLM gives you the ability to break away from relying solely on Linear Income without having to deal with a ton of risk. Get rid of fear, and get out of just making Traditional Income.

3.3 Residual Income

Residual Income is what leads to Freedom. There are 2 Types of Freedom that everyone wants to achieve:

1. Financial Freedom

2. Time Freedom

Imagine a life where you consistently had money coming in month after month whether you worked or not. Imagine the amount of Time Freedom that would afford you. Well, that's what Residual Income can lead to.

Residual Income is when you make money over and over again for work you've already performed. Residual Income also is what's known as "passive income," such as when you earn money from investments (your money making you more money).

There are 2 key ways to make residual income:

1. System (Efforts Of Other People)
2. Investments (Your Money Making You Money)

Now, imagine having other people and your money working harder for you to make you money than you do. That's what MLM offers you!

As you begin to sell products and then teach other people how to do the same, and begin to recruit a sales team and teach other people to do the same, you will begin to duplicate yourself. You will then begin to leverage your time. It's like you being in multiple places at one time. The Million Dollar Earners in the MLM/ Network Marketing Industry dedicate themselves to being the best at this. They focus most of their energies on "duplicating" themselves. If you want to be a Million Dollar MLM Earner, you should immediately start focusing on doing the same.

As Art Jonak put it:

"If you understood residual income, you would walk through a brick wall to get it."

This book is the "Shortcut" you've been waiting for to not just walk through a brick wall, but to knock the brick wall down!

3.4 Want Freedom More Than Security

Now that you understand the importance of Residual Income, you have to make the conscious decision to do everything in your power to achieve it. This starts with and ends with wanting Freedom more than Security.

Most people are concerned with having "security." This thought process typically never allows them to achieve Financial Success. I had a mentor early on tell me **"Most people want security, and I know where they can get maximum security... in a prison."**

What you must realize is that if you desire Security more than FREEDOM, you will build a wall around yourself and literally keep yourself from becoming Free. You'll be in a "Financial Prison." It's time for you to break the chains off of yourself and go for it! Desire FREEDOM with all you have in your innermost parts. I once heard, if you desire Freedom the way you would desire to breathe if your head was held under water, you will achieve it.

Focus on Freedom and teach others to do the same. This is a major attribute of all Million Dollar Earners in the MLM Industry. It's time for you to be FREE.

Chapter 4

FBS

4.1 What Is Your FBS?

What is your FBS? These initials stand for Financial Belief System.

Most people never stop to think about how they came to believe what they believe about making money. You had to learn it somewhere. Seriously, you had to learn about making money from somewhere or someone, didn't you? Well, where did you learn it from and who was it that taught you?

Literally, who taught you how to make money? I know I'm pounding on this point, but this is such a serious question that it deserves to be highlighted.

I ask this question to people practically every day. The response I receive usually goes something like this... "I don't know, I never thought about it."

Now stop for a moment and let me directly ask you the same question.

"Who Taught You How To Make Money?"

This is probably the most important question of your Financial Life thus far. I bet practically everyone reading this book has never been asked that question before.

When you honestly answer the question, most will be blown away as they scrape through their brains for an answer. I was asked this question in a similar manner in November of 1995, and it immediately changed my life!

I was challenged to take out a piece of paper and draw a line down the middle of it. I was then asked to write down the names of everyone I personally knew who was "Rich"" on the left side of the paper, and to write down the names of everyone I personally knew who was "broke and living paycheck to paycheck on the right side of the paper.

Wow! I scrambled as I tried to think of everyone I personally knew who was Rich. I came up with a handful of names. As I started to write down names of those that I personally knew who were broke, I quickly filled up the page. I would have needed a Notebook to complete the task of writing down the names of everyone I knew who was broke and living paycheck to paycheck. What a revelation.

The point was made. I then was challenged to listen to people who had the results that I wanted. I was asked... "Do you want to be Financially Free?" Of course, I answered "YES!"

Now, I'll ask you the same thing... "Do you want to be Financially Free?" I believe you would answer absolutely "YES." As in my case, you should be willing to do what I did and follow people who have a Financial Belief System that produces massive amounts of Residual Income. This is what ALL the Million Dollar MLM Earners know and understand. They all know that following financial principles that work is the only way.

This book is teaching you how to have the right Financial Belief System. Now it's up to you to put these philosophies to work.

4.2 Rid Yourself Of Other People's Opinions (OPO)

98% of the population fail miserably at obtaining Financial Independence. Their Financial Belief System has mostly been shaped by other people who are not Financially Independent.

Most of this "shaping" comes in the form of "OPO" (Other People's Opinions). If you are going to be a Multi-Million Dollar Producer in the MLM Industry, then you literally are going to have to "rid yourself from other people's opinions." I can promise you that these opinions are coming your way, and most of them are not going to be for your benefit.

It's easy to understand why most of these opinions will not be for your benefit. Here's why: Because most of the opinions coming to you are from others who don't have what you want.

When you settle in on this fact, you will be able to put yourself in a bracket that very few obtain. You will be able to think and act for yourself. Million Dollar Earners in the MLM Industry are almost "allergic" to the opinions of others who don't have what they want. They developed this skill before they made the millions. If you want to build a Multi-Million Dollar MLM Business, then you better quickly develop this skill as well. Rid yourself of OPO, then you will be able to grow.

You're always going to find people offering you opinions about your MLM Business. I've found that most of these opinions have the underlying tone of "jealousy" tied to them. Just imagine if you become a Millionaire through MLM/Network Marketing and they're stuck in a job. How do you think they will feel? They're going to feel stupid for trying to stop you.

I kept this in mind when I was starting my MLM Business in 1995. For all those who said I wouldn't make it, I just pictured how stupid they would feel when I did make it. I pictured the scene of me walking into a place where they were at and simply smiling and minding my business. I knew that when they saw me, other people would have already shared with them that I knocked the MLM Business "Out of the Park!" I wouldn't have to say a word, but inside I would be cracking up. Guess what? That's how it is now. I just crack up inside at those who tried to tear me down with their opinions who are still stuck at their jobs.

So, when someone wants to offer you their opinion ask them to offer to pay your bills if you accept their opinions. Guess what the response to that is going to be… "Yeah, right!" You can simply say… "That's what I thought."

Focus on listening to people who have what you want. This book is a great place to start.

4.3 Trust Yourself

Another important part of developing a strong FBS (Financial Belief System) is learning to trust and believe in yourself. You have to become your #1 Fan immediately.

I have a website titled "Quotes To Make You Better" where I release daily quotes as they come to me first thing in the morning. My "creative side of my brain" works best first thing in the morning, so I decided to take some of the first thoughts that come to me in the morning and publish them as quotes. This chapter about "Trust Yourself" reminds me of one of those quotes:

You need to become your #1 Fan immediately. This is another key trait of the Million Dollar Earners in the MLM Industry. They encourage themselves more than anybody else does. They learned to trust themselves quickly, which enables them to make quicker and more definite decisions. That doesn't mean all the decisions they make are correct. It means that they understand that they have to test themselves by making decisions. The more decisions they test, the better they get at making decisions. This is a refreshing way to look at making decisions. You need to become your own best counsel.

Most people are looking for someone else to validate them. This is what got most into the tough financial spot they're in now. They keep looking for others to validate them, not knowing others are pushing a Financial Belief System on them that they surely don't want. I mean, how many people want to be broke and living paycheck to paycheck?

It's time for you to trust yourself. You have enough common sense to tell what's right from wrong. You have the ability to listen to the sound advice of others who have what you want and come to your own conclusions to follow that advice or not. Following sound advice from documented MLM Professionals allows you to develop the strength to develop your own systems. This will then enable you to build a strong Financial Belief System.

Start trusting yourself today. You will do better, feel better, and be better.

4.4 Invest In Yourself

Another key component to developing a strong FBS (Financial Belief System) is "Investing In Yourself." You need to be wise with your money. One of the wisest things that the Million Dollar MLM Earners did to get where they are at now was to invest in personal growth resources. This book is a great place to start. As you are reading this book you are growing personally. I share a lot of Million Dollar MLM Information on my website www.JayNolandMLM.com to keep you growing and staying sharp. I have many FREE resources for you to take advantage of as well, but don't be afraid to spend money on becoming stronger.

The stronger you are the stronger your Financial Belief System will be. There are many other great Personal Growth Trainers that you can tap into and learn from as well. Trainers such as the great late Jim Rohn and Zig Ziglar have always been not only great Personal Growth Trainers, but they've been avid supporters of the MLM Industry as well. Other great Personal Growth Trainers that support the MLM Industry are Robert Kiyosaki, Les Brown, Brian Tracy, and Darren Hardy to name a few.

Start collecting a library of Personal Growth Trainings. Instead of listening to the radio all the time when you drive, one of the best things you can do is listen to Personal Growth CD's. I attribute listening to Personal Growth CD's to a great deal of my success. For nearly my first 2 years in the MLM Business I rarely listened to anything in my car other than Personal Growth CD's. Every minute I spent listening to Personal Growth CD's made me stronger and stronger. It will do the same for you too. Strong people build strong teams.

And, of course, EVERYONE needs to invest in the book "Think and Grow Rich." This is the #1 Success Book of all time. The book is written by Dr. Napoleon Hill. He did a 20+ year research on Financially Successful People and Financially Unsuccessful People. The book "Think and Grow Rich" is a condensed version of what he learned. I recommend you start with this book first in your Personal Growth journey. This book will for sure strengthen your FBS (Financial Belief System). You will be amazed at your transformation.

Chapter 5

Maximizing People

5.1 Where Does Money Grow?

When I talk about "Maximizing People," I'm talking about getting the most potential out of everybody you deal with. You want your relationships and interactions to be meaningful. There's no need to waste a lot of time. You're here to learn how to build a Multi-Million Dollar Business and you want to get the "Shortcut" in order to do so. A very powerful understanding you must have then, is learning "Where Does Money Grow?" This is one of the more critical parts of your training, so pay close attention.

Most of us have heard the saying that "Money Doesn't Grow On Trees!" The problem is that no one ever actually told us where Money does grow. You probably never thought about this, huh?

So let's ask the question again:

"Where Does Money Grow?"

Money grows in OTHER PEOPLE'S POCKETS!

Money comes from other people of all races, genders, creeds, religions, and demographics. Exchanging products and services for money from other people is the key to making profits. You have to quickly understand this philosophy right away in order to build any significant success in MLM. Knowing that those who exchange products and services for money from other people will make more money is the first key. The second key is knowing that you have to attract people and have them give you money. Those who attract the most people end up making the most money. Those who teach other people to attract more people have the potential to make Millions of Dollars in the MLM Industry.

I did a Blog Article titled "The Color of Money: Multiracial." This blog shares how money comes from all different types of people from all over the world. Take the time to read the article as it will open your eyes to a entirely different way at looking at money.

This philosophy has helped me build sales organizations that number over 500,000 Distributors in more than 50+ Countries throughout my career.

You can go to my website at www.JayNolandMLM.com and type in type in the search box "The Color of Money: Multiracial" to read the article, or you can go to it directly at:

http://www.jaynolandmlm.com/the-color-of-money-multiracial/

My mission is to help you explode your MLM Business and put you on the solid track to build it to become a Multi-Million Dollar business. Understanding where money comes from will help you get there faster. This understanding of "Where Does Money Grow" truly helps you "Maximize People."

5.2 Four (4) Percentages Of People

If you're going to "Maximize People" on your way to building a Multi-Million Dollar MLM/Network Marketing Business, then you have to get a good understanding of the different groups of people you are going to be running into. My close to 20 years of experience has taught me that there are 4 Percentages of People. This is another extremely important part of your training, so continue to pay close attention.

Here's the breakdown of each of the groups of people:

1. 27%'ers

2. 60%'ers
3. 10%'ers
4. 3%'ers

Let's go over each of the groups so you'll know who you're dealing with as you start Recruiting and Selling Your Products.

27%'ers

27'ers are what I label as "Unmotivatables." These are negative people whose entire mission is to bring as many people as possible into their miserable world. I'm not sure what made these people the way they are, but they are whom they are. Trying to motivate these people is absolutely useless. They have concluded that "life sucks," and they want to see how much life they can "suck" out of other people. If you are going to build a Multi-Million MLM Business then you have to avoid these people at all costs. 27%'ers are tricky at times though, because they will even sign up in your business with the intention of tearing down other people. Get rid of them. Don't try to change them, because it's virtually impossible. If you try to prove this wrong, you will definitely regret it. I want to save you some pain.

60%'ers

This is the vast majority of the people that you will run into. I label 60%'ers as "Motivatables". This group of people are easily swayed by typically anything they hear. If they hear something good, then they are excited. If someone tells them something negative, then they get down. This group of people are all over the place and can drive you nuts when it comes to building the business. I know these people very well, because when I started in the MLM Industry in 1995, I was one of them. I used to go up and down all the time until I met this wonderful industry of MLM. I'm very thankful for my early upline leaders and mentors helping me to understand that I couldn't get anywhere significant going up and down. The same goes for you and those you recruit. You can't go anywhere significant going up and down.

10%'ers

10'ers are what I label as "Self-Motivated." The label clearly describes this group. They motivate themselves. They don't need anyone to encourage them. If they see a good opportunity and they have the time, they take advantage of it. You don't have to tell a 10%'er to do something twice. They do what needs to be done. You also don't have to chase a 10%'er. 10%'ers are refreshing to be around, because they don't go up and down. "10'ers" are those who will become your best leaders.

3%'ers

At the top of the "money chain" is the 3%'ers. These are who I label the "Motivators." 3%'ers know how to motivate and move others. This is the ultimate goal for anyone who is reading this book. A 3%'er spends "zero time" with a 27%'er. A 3%'er quickly establishes guidelines with a 60%'er to encourage them to quickly become a 10%'er. If a 3%er sees a 60%'er going up and down, they will encourage them a maximum of 2 times. After that, a 3%'er will move on. 3%'ers spend the majority of their time developing 60%'ers to become 10%'ers and 10%'ers to become Great Leaders in order to become 3%ers as well. Those outside of the MLM Industry who are 3%'ers typically won't join your opportunity because they're typically already Financially Free. They will, however, typically support you by being a wholesale customer and possibly giving you referrals. 3%'ers in MLM are not born, they are built. You can be a 3%'er too, but you have to be willing to stay the course and go through the ups and downs with a great attitude on your way.

I broke these groups down in detail in a blog article on my website at www.JayNolandMLM.com. The Article is titled "3%, 10%, 60%, 27% (Which One Are You?)." You can type the name of the article in the "search box," or you can go to the link directly at:

http://www.jaynolandmlm.com/3-10-60-27-which-one-are-you/

Now, when you are recruiting you will be able to quickly notice which group your recruit fits into. Focus on finding 10%'ers. Approximately half of them will join your opportunity if you are at least a 10%'er yourself. This means that if you are a 60%'er now, you need to immediately make the change. You can do it. What I've just shared with you is worth Millions of Dollars. Pay attention, apply this information, and watch your Recruiting Efforts and MLM Business SOAR!

5.3 Four (4) Personality Types Of People

The next stage in learning the skill of "Maximizing People" is understanding the 4 Personality Types of People. Every person has each of the 4 Personality Types in them but typically 2 of them are more dominant. It usually takes a lot of time to master dealing with each of these 4 personality types. I have detailed training material on this subject that will be coming out soon (it may already be available when you read this... check the online store at www.jaynolandmlm.com). The key here with this book is to make sure you are aware of each of these Personality Types so that you are able to attract more people. Trust me. This is a major Million Dollar MLM Shortcut when you master this skill.

Here's a breakdown of each of the 4 Personality Types:

1. Cause Motivated
2. Fun Motivated
3. Analytically Motivated
4. Money Motivated

Let's go over each of the Personality Types, so you'll know who you're dealing with when you are Recruiting.

Cause Motivated

Cause Motivated Personality Types are driven by things that have a cause and a deeper purpose to it. These folks are not motivated by "money first." They have to really believe in what they are doing. They have to feel that there is a "greater good" coming from what they are doing. For example, if there is a "Non-Profit Organization" that benefits from their efforts, then they will be more motivated. Cause motivated people like to have "deep conversations." They are also very caring people.

Fun Motivated

Fun Motivated Personality Types are extremely driven by things that are FUN. If they can't have fun, then they don't really want to do it. They will do just about anything if there is fun involved. These folks are very "social" and attract a lot of people. They are typically not very organized as they feel organization takes away from the fun of things. They hate having to deal with analytical things whatsoever. They are very spontaneous.

Analytically Motivated

Analytically Motivated Personality Types are driven by the

exact details of things. Their definition of "fun" is figuring out how things work. They love the science behind things. The more detailed information they can get, the more satisfied they are. These folks are typically the "brains" behind the project. They don't need a lot of recognition. They want things done on time. They are very organized people.

Money Motivated

Money Motivated Personality Types are typically very aggressive. Their number one concern is making money. If they can't make money doing it, they don't want to do it. These folks don't need to know how everything works as long as it produces a result that leads to making more money. Money Motivated people are very competitive. They don't like anyone beating them at anything. They are also very "goal oriented" people.

From this point forward, be sure in your recruiting efforts to share information that will motivate the person based on their personality type.

For example: If you notice that they are FUN going people, talk to them about how they will get to meet so many fun and outgoing people in your company. Also, talk about the events and travel involved with your company. If they seem to be MONEY motivated, focus on your company's compensation plan. If they are CAUSE motivated, show them how your company is supporting great causes. If they are ANALYTICAL, guide them to as much literature as possible about your company's products and compensation plan.

Everyone has all 4 of these personality traits in them, but remember that most people are typically dominate in 2 of the 4 Personality Types. Knowing this information will truly help you in "Maximizing People."

Most people have no clue about what you've just learned, so you now have a major advantage. Million Dollar Earners in the MLM Industry are masters at identifying and relating to these 4 Personality Types. You need to do the same on your way to building a Multi-Million Dollar MLM Business.

5.4 OPI, OPM, OPE

"Maximizing People" means you must utilize "leverage" as much as possible. The most effective "leverage" you can utilize is OPI, OPM, and OPE.

- OPI = Other People's Ideas
- OPM = Other People's Money
- OPE = Other People's Efforts

Let's break each of these down:

OPI (Other People's Ideas)

You don't have to "reinvent the wheel." The power of the MLM Industry is that companies figure out how to create a great product, a great compensation plan, and a great infrastructure for you. MLM Owners come up with great ideas and allow distributors to profit from their ideas if they market the company's products. The better you market as a distributor, the more you leverage "Other People's Ideas." You get to leverage the MLM Owner's "ideas" as if they were your own. All you have to do is focus primarily on marketing and recruiting, and the rest is pretty much done for you.

OPM (Other People's Money)

Most MLM Owners have to invest Millions of Dollars on all

the various aspects of the company. As a distributor, you don't have to put up Millions of Dollars, yet it's as if you did when you join the company. In most cases, you literally get to leverage the Millions of Dollars already spent developing the company and its products. You get to become a "capitalist" when you join a MLM Company. This means you get to exchange money with other people for your company's products and you get to keep the Profit. The power of leveraging "Other People's Money" cannot be underestimated. The more you take advantage of the Millions your company has already spent, the more you are leveraging "Other People's Money."

OPE (Other People's Efforts)

Leveraging "Other People's Efforts" means you get to build a TEAM. You no longer have to be the only one responsible for your income. Without a team helping you make money, it's nearly impossible to become Financially Free. You can leverage the energy and efforts of other people every time you recruit someone to become a distributor on your team. When you teach your team members to recruit others to become distributors you are maximizing the leverage of "Other People's Efforts."

Chapter 6

Million Dollar MLM Techniques

6.1 Retail Sales

One of the most overlooked components in building a Multi-Million Dollar MLM Business is the power of Retail Sales. Retail Sales involves building a real Retail Customer Base for your products. The MLM Industry officially began in 1945. A company called "Nutrilite" created the first documented compensation plan. The essence of the plan was that a Distributor could purchase produce from the company at a 35% Discount and then sell the products to others at Retail Pricing. Not until the Distributor could acquire 25 Customers would they be allowed to "Sponsor" someone else and develop a team.

Somewhere between 1945 and now, most of the industry has missed the power of Retail Sales. One of the most important reasons for my success in generating approximately 2 Billion Dollars in Sales in just a handful of years is that I make sure to teach my teams the power of Retail Sales. Some of your best Distributors will be someone who was a "Satisfied Retail Customer" first. What I love about Retail Sales is that it allows a new Distributor to "stay in the game" while they're learning how to consistently recruit other distributors.

Retail Sales also provides more validation and confidence for your team members (especially new distributors) that the business works, because it provides instant profit. Remember, capitalism is the exchange of products and services for PROFIT.

Out of 100% of your sales team, approximately 80% will simply focus on "Supplementing Their Income." You'll have approximately 10% who will focus on "Replacing Their Income" (Getting Out Of The JOB). Then you'll have another 10% who will focus on "Financial Freedom" (Getting Rich). Believe it or not, as time goes by, if you are able to build a Long Term Multi-Million Dollar MLM Business, you will find that most of your income will come from the 80% Group of Distributors on your team who are simply "Supplementing Their Income."

The Million Dollar MLM Earners know this to be true. Retail Sales is the foundation of how the Industry was started in the first place. You buy products from your company at wholesale pricing and sell the products at retail pricing. The difference between the wholesale and retail price is your Retail Profit. Having great "consumable" products and services increases your chance of repeat sales. This also increases your chances of having one of your Retail Customers becoming a Distributor once they fall in love with the products. When people love something, they talk to others about it. This then becomes natural Network Marketing.

I like for those that I work with to focus on obtaining at least a 100 Retail Customer Base. I know many may be thinking "How in the world would I have time to service and deliver products to all those people?" This thought is what stops most distributors from focusing on Retail Sales, but I'm going to teach you how to deal with this right now.

In my 20 years of experience, I've found that the average Retail Customer is worth approximately $50 per month in Retail Profit (if you've got great consumable products and services with your company). If you've got 100 Retail Customers that will mean you're making about $5,000 per month in Retail Profit. This is more than the average person working a Full-Time Job earns! If you take a portion of that Profit (say $500 - $1,000 per month) and pay a High School Student to deliver your products and service your Retail Customers, you still have $4,000 - $4,500 per month in Retail Profit. On top of this, you'll probably have a consistent amount of Retail Customers either becoming Preferred Customers or Distributors on your team, because you've got a ton of exposure in the marketplace with your products from having so many Retail Customers.

Retail Sales are simple to do too. A great way to get your Retail Sales going is to utilize contacts you already know. I'll show you a simple approach to developing quick Retail Sales, and this gets everyone's confidence up right away as well. Here's a Retail Script of what to say to your personal contacts to start developing quick Retail Sales (Profits):

Retail Sales Script

"Hello, _____ (name of your friend or family member). Small talk for a few seconds, then get to the purpose of the call (to sell your products).

"_____(name of your friend or family member), I need your **help**. The reason for my call is that I just started a new business and have some excellent products (or services). I need your help... I would like to have you as one of my first key customers by buying a product or two (or service) from me at retail one time. If you like it I will show you how to get the products (or services) at wholesale, but if you don't like it, I will never ask you to buy from me again. Will you do me a favor and **help me out** by buying a product or two (or service) at least one time?"

They will ask how much does it cost and you tell them:
"It's only "x amount" Retail per product (or service). This breaks down to as little as "x amount" per serving (or you can say "x amount" per day) . If you like it, I will show you how to get it at wholesale from now on, and you'll really be doing me a huge favor helping me get my business started. How many [Name of Your Products (or services) would you like to buy and help me out?"

Take the order and then ask for referrals.

**Always ask who else do they know who may be interested in your products/services that you can share the products/services with. If they give you referrals that buy, then tell them you will give them a discount the next time they decide to purchase from you.

For people you don't know that you run into or prospect here's all you need to do:

1. Get excited about your company's products!
2. Sample Your Product or Services. (Let people smell, taste, see, try.)
3. Get excited again! (Get your customers' emotions involved.)
4. Tell Stories. (Testimonials of other people's success with your product. It's a good idea to have a "Testimonial Book" to show.)
5. Give Multiple Choice Options. (Do you want 1, 2, or 3 of my products/services?)
6. Smile. (After you give Multiple Choice Options, don't talk. Let them make a decision.)

By doing the above 6 Steps over and over, and utilizing your training on the "numbers," you are more than likely going to develop a good Retail Customer Base. Be sure to develop a Retail Customer "List" so that you can keep track of your customers (remember the importance of tracking).

Now you have solid training on Retail Sales and developing a Retail Customer Base. Don't overlook this very important part of developing your Multi-Million Dollar MLM Business.

6.2 Recruiting

Most every distributor in MLM wants to become an awesome

Recruiter. Most distributors want the feeling of having a large team that they can lead. Just imagine the feeling of accomplishment if you have thousands of people on your team. Imagine having 10,000 or maybe even 50,000 distributors on your team. What a powerful feeling that would be, wouldn't it?

I'm here to tell you it's possible. If I can do it coming from a small town in Kentucky and primarily growing up on a farm, then you can do it. I didn't have a clue about Financial Success or how o Recruit. I learned how to and you can too.

In order to build a large team, you're going to have to learn how to "Recruit." If you apply the teachings in the previous chapters you'll be well on your way to being a Great Recruiter. This chapter will cover some of the exact techniques to put it all together for you.

One of the number one things you have to have in order to be a Great Recruiter is a "Pleasant Personality." Remember, money comes from other people. You have to "attract" people who want to be around you. No matter how passionate you are, if people feel like you are a "jerk," they're not going to want to be around you. I'm not telling you that you have to please everybody. I'm telling you to be pleasant. Be focused and driven, but be pleasant. This is another major trait of the Million Dollar Earners in the MLM Industry.

Now that we've got that down, let's talk about some specific techniques to become a Great Recruiter.

A. Recruit From The HEART

Great Recruiters recruit from the <u>HEART</u>. They believe in what they are doing so deeply that it is easy to convey that to others. If you can't believe in your product or your company that you're with, then it's not going to work. You have to feel a deep burning desire to share your opportunity with other people. You literally have to feel that your opportunity will save their financial life. If you can convey this type of belief, then others will begin to respond. People are looking for someone to lead. People will follow someone who is deeply convinced about what they are doing and where they are going, so make the decision to Recruit from the HEART from this point forward.

B. Different Approaches

There are different approaches when it comes to Recruiting, but primarily there are 2:

1. 1 on 1's
2. Group Presentations

The key with both of these is to "Set Appointments." Your recruiting focus should always be on setting appointments, whether it's "1 on 1's" or "Group Presentations."

C. Groups of People

There 2 different groups of people you will be Recruiting in order to "Set Appointments":

1. Warm Market (People You Know)
2. Cold Market (People You Don't Know)

Warm Market

Your Warm Market is composed of 3 Groups. Here's the 3 Groups and the approaches to use with them:

A. People You're Equal To

People who've achieved about the same success as you have thus far in life, you want to ask them for a **FAVOR** to look at your opportunity.

B. People You Look Up To
People who've achieved more success than you thus far in life, you want to ask them for an **OPINION** to look at your opportunity

C. People Who Look Up To You
People who've achieved less success than you thus far in life, you want to **TELL** them to look at your opportunity and get started.

Keep in mind that it doesn't matter what you think about who has reached the most success thus far in life. In Recruiting, it only matters what they think. If they think they've achieved more success in life than you have, let them be right. Your goal is to set an appointment and get them to see the opportunity.

Once you set the appointment, then you will use the steps outlined in the following chapters (6.3-6.7) in order to get your prospects involved in the business.

Cold Market

Your Cold Market is comprised of people that you don't know. You may run into these people when you are out and about. You may meet some of these folks over the phone. Either way, I'll provide you with a simplified approach at Recruiting these prospects with the entire focus on "Setting An Appointment."

When you meet a Cold Market Prospect:

A. Compliment Them

Example: You meet someone in a Retail Store. Say "You know what, with the way you carry yourself, you must be the manager here..." Most of the time they will say something like "Yeah right, I'm not the manager, but I wish I was..."

B. Ask if they keep their career options open

Example: After complimenting them, say something like, "Well, you should be the manager... "By the way, do you keep your career options open?"

C. Tell them you can't make any promises

Example: After asking if they keep their career options open, say something like, "Listen, my company is rapidly expanding and looking for some good people to help with the expansion. I can't make you any promises, but I can set you up with an appointment to see if we get a match... how's that sound?" (Most people will be excited about something new with more potential than where they are at.)

D. Get their cell phone number and email

Example: After telling them you can't make any promises, pull out a pen and a piece of paper. Put your pen to the paper and don't look up. Then ask, "What's your cell number and email where I can follow up with you to set the appointment?" If you don't look up, they'll give you their cell number and email 99% of the time. Don't set the appointment at that time. Follow up with them to set the appointment. It's important that you look busy and have things to do. Get the information and then move on.

E. Follow up and set the appointment

Example: Within 24 hours, call them to set the appointment. If they ask for details over the phone, let them know it's important that they make the appointment to get all the exact details. Don't get into details over the phone. Set an appointment.

Once you set the appointment, then you will use the steps outlined in the following chapters (6.3-6.7) in order to get your prospects involved in the business.

Again, the key to both Warm Market and Cold Market Recruiting is to "Set Appointments." Recruiting is a "contact business." I call it B2B (Body to Body). You have to meet with people. You have to develop relationships.

You can use the Internet to Recruit (Online Marketing Systems, Squeeze Pages, Lead Services, etc), but at the end of the day, you still are going to have to personally interact with people and develop relationships if you want to build a long term Multi-Million Dollar MLM Business. I've seen many so-called "experts" try to guide people into believing that they can build an MLM Business using solely the Internet and not have to talk to people. This may work for a short run, but will not last long term. Why? If some other online marketing campaign comes along and sounds better, your distributors will jump ship and join another company. It happens all the time.

When you Recruit and focus on building Personal Relationships, this creates a bond and loyalty. When you have a strong bond with your team members and strong loyalty, you will be able to stand the test of time. It's worth it for you to learn how to build relationships in order to build a long term Multi-Million Dollar MLM Business.

Now you've received solid training on Recruiting to develop a long term business. If you use these steps correctly, you will be on your way to building a Multi-Million Dollar MLM Business that can last.

6.3 Seven (7) Step Powerful Presentation

Now it's time to put your training thus far into action. The first action step you want to focus on is doing a great presentation. You need to practice, practice, practice. Most that get into MLM have no clue about the philosophy behind doing a great presentation. You will now have the true and tried steps that have generated Billions of Dollars in Sales Volume throughout my career. I call this the 7 Step Power Presentation.

Let's breakdown each of the steps:

1. **Intro: About You (2-3 mins)**

   A. Your Name
   B. Where you're from
   C. What you currently or used to do for work
   D. What the *Company* means to you and where you see your future going with your company

2. **Company: (3-5 mins)**

   A. Company's Founder and Executive Team
   B. Bullet Points of Company (Philosophy)

3. **Traditions and Industries (5-7 mins)**

   A. Plan A vs. Plan B (Job vs Business)
   a. Taught to go to school, get good grades, then get a job.

VERSUS

b. Build a Successful MLM Business (Residual Income).
c. Successful Business is based on capitalizing on Trends - Go over the industry or industries that your MLM Company is involved in (ex: Health & Wellness, Weight Loss, Telecommunications, Skin Care, etc).

4. Products (5 - 7 mins)

A. Go over your Company's Product Line and Benefits (don't get overly detailed).

5. Compensation Plan (5 - 7 mins)

A. Go over the significant highlights of your Company's compensation plan.
B. Give some "Simple Theoretical Examples" of how the payout works (be sure to state there are no guarantees to success).

6. Training/Testimonials (7-10 mins)

A. Go over the types of Training and Support your Company and Team provides. Assure your prospects they will not be left alone.
B. If possible, have 2 or 3 people give a quick Testimonial about the positives of your Company's products and business opportunity.

7. Close: Sorting 3 Types of People (3-5 mins)

A. Customers. (Retail or Preferred Customer. Would like to try to the product to see how it works)
B. Needs More Information.

C. Ready to start making either Supplemental Income, Replacement Income (No More Job), or Financial Freedom (Get Rich).

Entire 7 Step Presentation should be between 30-45 minutes (45 minutes MAX!)

IMPORTANT: After Presentation Go Through **4 Steps To Success** focusing primarily on the 2nd and 3rd Type People (B's and C's).

*We cover 4 Steps to Success in the next chapter.

The key is to go through as many 7 Step Power Presentations as possible with as many prospects as possible. Remember, "The Numbers Tell The Whole Story." The more people you show the 7 Step Power Presentation to, the more people you will sponsor and the more product you will sell.

6.4 Four (4) Steps To Success

After you've taken people through the 7 Step Power Presentation, you want to take them through the "4 Steps to Success." The 4 Steps to Success is what actually closes the sale on sponsoring new prospects. Companies and Upline Leaders may differ somewhat on this process. Focus on working with your Company's or your Upline Leader's closing process if they are producing good results.

If there is not a closing system in place with your Company or Upline, then I suggest you immediately use the "4 Steps to Success." I've used these same 4 Steps to Success for 20 years, and they've helped me generate Billions of Dollars in Sales. They can help you build a solid business too.

4 Steps to Success

Step 1: Get Started (Fill out Application/Pick a Product Package)

A. Display the different options for a person to get started
B. Let the prospects know the different benefits that come with getting started (i.e. amount of product per each package, website, back office, etc)

Step 2: Be a Product of the Product

A. Use the products and pay attention to the difference you feel. If you are selling a service, you need to use the service and notice how it improved your life.
B. Be a product of the business success system that your company has to make money right away.
C. Develop your product and you business success story.
D. As soon you get a result (product or business), send your "Written Testimonial" to your Sponsor and the Company (this helps you take "possession and ownership" of your opportunity).

Step 3: Build a Team

A. Make a List (Share Product and Opportunity with Others)
B. Start with your Cell Phone. Also use a Memory Jogger Form. (Fill Out Immediately.) Write down at least 200 Contacts.
C. Everyone you know should at least buy one product from you to help you start Your Business.
D. Some people will just use the products (Retail or Preferred Customer).
E. Some people will want to build the Business (Take

them through a Presentation and have them choose a Package).

F. Make a List of Your Top 5 Dreams. (This is what will keep you on track to your success when you go through tough times.)

Step 4: Pay Attention to the Training & Duplicate

A. Let people know that they will need to commit to paying attention to the training, because the Company's training can show them how to make the money they really want. They need to also commit to duplicating the training with as many people as possible.

There are multiple types of training and support available such as:

- Personal Coaching
- Conference Calls
- Webinars
- 800# Info
- Live Presentations and Training
- Corporate Events

4 Steps to Success should take between 30-45 mins MAX.

The more people that you take through the *4 Steps to Success*, the more money you will make and help others make!

6.5 Seven (7) Steps to Duplication

Now that you have the 7 Step Powerful Presentation and the 4 Steps to Success training, you need to start Recruiting. The key to building a Multi-Million Dollar MLM Business is Duplication. You have to "Duplicate Yourself" as much as possible. This is done by taking people through a 7 Step Process and Tracking each person you personally recruit. It would be a good idea to create a Notebook for tracking your prospects. Every time you prospect someone, write their name at the top of a sheet of paper and then see how many of the 7 Steps you can take them through. If you can get someone all the way through the 7 Steps, then you've duplicated yourself.

Here are the **7 Steps to Duplication:**

1. **Invite**
   - Nothing happens if you don't first invite someone to see the opportunity.
2. **Show Up**
   - They have to show up to see the Presentation.
3. **See It**
   - This means that the opportunity makes sense to them.
4. **Get Started**
   - They have to fill out and Application and get some product or services (preferably a product package).
5. **Product of the Product**
   - They have to use the product or services and send you and the Company their testimonial, ideally within 48 hours. It's doesn't matter how big or small their results are. The most important thing is for them to share some type of Testimonial right away.
6. **Build a Team**
   - They have to immediately start working on building a team. They need to write out at least 200 Names ideally within 48 hours. They need to start contacting people with the help of yourself, your upline, or scripts right away, and selling them products or inviting them to see a presentation.

They need to also make a list of their Top 5 Dreams and share a copy with you. You can then help keep them focused on building their business by attaching their dreams to the business.

7. Pay Attention to the Training & Duplicate

- They have to be willing to Pay Attention to the Training and Duplicate it.

Now that you have the "7 Steps to Duplication," you need to focus on taking as many people as possible through these 7 Steps. In order for them to be "truly duplicated," they have to do each step in full. You'll notice the "4 Steps to Success" are included in the 7 Steps to Duplication. This keeps the process simple for you and your team to duplicate.

Also, notice that you have the most control over Step #1 (Invite). The more you turn up your "Inviting," the more the rest of the steps will fall into place. You also have already been trained in the prior chapters on how to stay focused on the "numbers" as well as the attitude you need. In the next chapter, we're going to focus a bit more on Duplication Step #1 (Invite). This is a critical part of your success when it comes to recruiting new prospects. You're on your way to building a Multi-Million Dollar MLM Business.

6.6 Recruit to Invite vs. Invite to Recruit

One of the most important lessons you'll learn in Recruiting is the difference between "Recruit to Invite vs. Invite to Recruit." Keeping in mind the key to building a Multi-Million Dollar MLM Business is "duplication." Without duplication, your dreams of building a Multi-Million Dollar MLM Business will simply be in vain.

"Recruit to Invite" is a principle you must master, and it's best to master this early on in your MLM Career before you develop bad habits. Look closely at the words RECRUIT to INVITE. You want to get awesome at "Recruiting INVITERS!"

Most people are excited about Inviting someone to Recruit them. The Million Dollar Earners in the MLM Industry really only get excited when their new enrollee INVITES someone else to a Presentation and begins the process of the 7 Steps to Duplication. Keep this mindset as your focus, and you will leverage the efforts of other people the way the powerhouse producers in the MLM Industry do.

I broke down "Recruit to Invite vs. Invite to Recruit" in detail in a blog article on my website at **www.JayNolandMLM.com**. The Article is titled "One Will Make You, The Other Will Break You." You can type the name of the article in the "search box" when you get to website, or you can go to the link directly at:

http://www.jaynolandmlm.com/one-will-make-you-the-other-will-break-you/

Being a "Great Recruiter" means you need to become an awesome "Inviter" as well as recruiting other awesome "Inviters."

6.7 F.O.R.M.

Typically, one of the most awkward moments when someone shows up for a Presentation is knowing what to say before the Presentation begins. The worst mistake you could make is trying to explain everything before the Presentation begins. This kills the "edification" for the Speaker. This also kills a lot of the "energy" in the Presentation. It's like someone trying to explain a movie before the movie begins. Really, who likes that person?

There is a simple process for talking with your prospects before the Presentation begins that I've used for almost 2 decades that works perfectly. This also increases your "Closing Ratio" as you know more about your prospect and what you need to say to get them started in your business.

Each letter in F.O.R.M. stands for what you need to be talking about before the Presentation. Here's the breakdown of F.O.R.M.:

The "F" in F.O.R.M

The "F" in F.O.R.M stands for "Family and Friends." When your prospect shows up, simply start asking about their Family and Friends. Ask questions like where they are from, are they married, do they have any kids, how old are the kids, how is their family doing, what's new and exciting in their life, etc. If you already know this person, simply catch up with how their family and friends are doing.

The "O" in F.O.R.M

The "O" in F.O.R.M stands for "Occupation." Ask your prospect about what they are doing for work or what they use to do for work. Next ask these 2 critical questions: What do they like MOST about their current or previous job/occupation; and secondly (be sure to ask this second), What do they like LEAST about their current or previous job/occupation. Take a strong mental note of each of these responses, so you can use them to sponsor them in the business when the Presentation is over.

The "R" in F.O.R.M

The "R" in F.O.R.M stands for "Recreation." You want to ask

them what they like to do for fun. Be sure to take a strong mental note of this response, so you can use the response to help sponsor them into the business when the Presentation is over.

The "M" in F.O.R.M

The "M" in F.O.R.M stands for "Money and Motivation." Ask what type of money they are use to making. Also ask if money were not an issue, what truly motivates them. Again, be sure to take strong mental notes of these responses, so you can use these to sponsor them into the business when the Presentation is over.

After you've gone through F.O.R.M. with your prospect, you are now prepared with all the information you'll need to get them sponsored into the business.

Here's an example to show you how to use F.O.R.M.

Let's say my prospect Tom shows up to the Presentation. I take him through F.O.R.M. (You don't tell them you're taking them through F.O.R.M., you just do it).

Let's say Tom tells me he's married and has 2 kids (boy and a girl) ages 7 and 9. He tells me that he'd love it if he can spend more time with his wife and kids.

He then tells me that he has been a Social Worker for 5 years. He then says what he likes most is dealing with people and helping to solve problems. He then says what he likes least is that he simply doesn't make enough money and spends too much time away from his family.

Next, he says that he loves to travel. He says he wants to travel to Europe with his family for an entire Summer but can't get that much time off from his job. He also says at this time and in the foreseeable future that he can't afford to make such a trip, but would love it.

Finally he tells me that he's making about $30,000 per year. He goes on to say that if money were not an issue, he'd love to start his own foundation to help the homeless.

Now, can you see how much information in that short period of time that I have to use to motivate Tom to get started in the business?

This will probably be a "slam dunk" if Tom is even half-way "open" to new ideas of making money.

Here's what I'd say when the Presentation was over. Now, I know some of you are on the edge of your seats wanting to know this information, huh? LOL!

Here it goes... I'd say:

"Tom, great presentation wasn't it? Tom, I'm sure you can see how us working together we could quickly get you to the point where you could spend more time with your wife and kids. I'm sure you also see how much of a people business this is, and someone with your skills could really help a lot of people. At the same time, you'll finally be rewarded for your skills of working with people as your income potential now will be "unlimited." What I'm most excited about for you Tom is seeing you finally being able to take that summer long vacation to Europe with your family and have more than enough money to do so. As a matter of fact, when you build this the right way, you'll have the Residual Income coming in even while you're on vacation. I know you mentioned that you're used to making $30,000 per year, but imagine the opportunity to make that per month. I'm not making you any guarantees of income, but

there are many people in this industry who make more than that. With the unlimited income potential you have working with our company, you'll be able to actually start your own Foundation to help out the homeless. You'll know where every penny is going in your Foundation, because you own it. Now, Tom it's time to get you on your way to making these things we've talked about a reality. None of this is possible without you getting started. So, Tom which Package do you see yourself getting started with? A, B, C, or D?"

If Tom comes back with any hesitation at all, I will simply continue to use the information he's given me in F.O.R.M to assist him in getting started. I will ask him... "How long will it take you at your current job to achieve what we just talked about here?"

I will be speaking from my heart, because I know what this industry can do. I learned early in my MLM career to truly care about helping people get what they want. So, I know I have to be strong for them in the beginning when it comes time for them to make the decision to get started.

If Tom is still hesitant or in "think about it" mode, I will <u>address his fears</u> with him. You see, I know that the opportunity I'm offering him is his way to his hopes and dreams. I know that if he doesn't get started he will probably never even come close to his dreams. Therefore, I'm willing to get in the "mental trenches" with Tom and help him, if need be, to see the "urgency" of the situation. His hopes and dreams are on the line. I've got the answer to his problem. If he truly wants his hopes and dreams to come true, **<u>he will get started</u>**.

Remember, if he's hesitant, he's probably a 60%'er and will need a little boost. If he's a 10%'er, he'll more than likely get started right away if he doesn't have any other major projects going on at that time.

ATTENTION!

What I've just shared with you is literally worth **Millions of Dollars**. There are very few people who know what I just taught you, and if they do know, most won't share their secrets. This is just the scratch of the scratch of the surface of the training that I can teach you about closing sales in the MLM Industry. Be sure to stay plugged into my training site at **www. JayNolandMLM.com.**

Now that you've got the F.O.R.M training and some very important "closing techniques," you are well on your way to having the right mindset of a Million Dollar MLM Earner. You just have to back your new mindset with action!

Chapter 7

Call To Action

7.1 Competence

We've covered a lot of information in this book. Very few people get the specifics of how to build a Multi-Million Dollar MLM Business like you've gotten from this book, let alone a "Shortcut." Now, you've got to put all you've learned into ACTION. You have to be willing to learn the MLM business inside and out. Embrace the opportunity to learn how to become a Top Producer in the MLM Industry. Learning comes from studying and putting what you learn into practice. As you learn more, your competence will increase. The higher your "competence" (capacity of knowledge), the more you will earn.

There are 4 stages of "competence" that every Million Dollar MLM Earner goes through. Knowing these stages will provide you with the confidence of knowing you will eventually master the MLM Industry.

Unconscious Incompetence: This is when you don't have any idea about what to do or how to do it. (Most don't have a clue about how MLM really works.)

Conscious Incompetence: This is when you "admit" that you don't have an idea about what to do or how to do it, but you're willing to learn. (This is the beginning of greatness.)

Conscious Competence: This is when you now know what to do, but you to have "consciously" think about it. (Now, you're on your way.)

Unconscious Competence: This is when you know what to do, and you do it naturally without even thinking about it. (Big Money Time)

Your mission should be to get to **"Unconscious Competence"** in the MLM Industry as fast as possible. I've given you the "Shortcut" on how to do it through this book, but you're now going to have to get out there and do it.

Have confidence that you will learn the MLM Industry inside and out. Have confidence that you will become a Multi-Million Dollar Producer. The only thing that can stop you from achieving this is you. I'm believing in you, right here and right now, to apply what you've learned in this book. There's no reason you can't become one of the best. Commit to taking massive action, and then go do it!

7.2 Immersion

To make the techniques in this book come to life for you, you're going to have to totally immerse yourself into applying everything here that you've learned.

Believe it or not, when I first got started in the industry, my mission was to make $20,000 in my first month. When I saw those "circles" on the board, I literally was amazed at the financial possibilities the industry of MLM had to offer. I literally wanted to run out the door and down the street shouting, "Yes, Yes... I've found what I've been looking for!" I thought that everyone would see and understand this industry. How funny for me to look back on that time now.

Well, I didn't make $20,000 in my first month. I only made about $3,200 in my first month, which is considered great by industry standards. However, this wasn't my standard. I sincerely wanted to make $20,000 in a month as fast as humanly possible. So, I went after it again my second month. I didn't hit it again. As a matter of fact, I went backwards and only made about $1,200.

My upline told me the reason I went backwards was because I wasn't paying attention to the training like I did my first month. She was right. So, I set after it again my third month. Again, I didn't hit it. I made about $3,000, which was at least better than my second month. However, I didn't hit my goal.

I was so focused to make $20,000 in one month that I challenged myself to not watch Television again until I did it. I thought to myself, surely, I will do it my fourth or fifth month (no longer than my sixth month).

Listen, I'm a sports fan. I love watching Baseball, Basketball, Football, Tennis, and Golf on Television. I just knew I wouldn't miss watching any major sports events (World Series, NBA and NCAA Championship, Super Bowl, Tennis and Golf Majors). I knew I'd hit my goal right away.

Well, it took me 15 more months to accomplish my goal of earning $20,000 in one month. In my 18th month I earned $24,000. I missed watching all the major sporting events for over a year. My question to you is... "Do you think it was worth it?" I'll answer it for you... ABSOLUTELY. My career took off from that point like a Rocket Ship.

I'm telling you this because I want you to understand the thought process of "immersing yourself" into your MLM Business so that you can literally take a "Shortcut" to tremendous success. Trust me. It's worth every bit of the sacrifice. I took longer to start earning the big money, but I eventually did it because I was immersed into the business. I've already figured out practically every way not to do the business right, so you can learn from my experience and take a "Shortcut."

You need to immerse yourself into the training that is available with your company. You need to immerse yourself into your company's compensation plan. You need to immerse yourself into selling as much product as possible. You need to immerse yourself into recruiting as many people as possible until you become great at it. You need to immerse yourself into personal growth trainings (CD's, DVD's, Live Events, etc). You simply need to go above and beyond and immerse yourself so that you can separate yourself from the masses.

Just keep telling yourself that it's worth it. Keep reminding yourself that you deserve success, because very few people are willing to pay the price you are paying.

Immersing yourself into your MLM Business will probably have some people that you are close to thinking that you're crazy and have lost your mind. It doesn't matter what they think (Remember OPO?). They are not going to pay your bills for you. It's not their hopes and dreams, it's yours. Go for it.

Chapter 8

Conclusion

8.1 Finishing Touch

I'm honored that you took the time to complete the reading of this book. I'm confident that you have been positively impacted, because I wrote this book from my heart. I don't know where I would be without the wonderful industry of MLM.

It's not just about the money I've made or the Lifestyle that I live. It really is about how much I've been able to grow personally. It's about the thousands upon thousands of lives I've been fortunate enough to positively impact.

I wish the same for you. I want you to have what you truly want out of this life You've got everything it takes to make it happen. The only thing that stands between your Million Dollar Success Story is you. If you bring the effort, you'll get the results.

The beautiful things about "effort" is that it is between you and you. No one else can give you "effort." No matter how powerful this information is in this book, if you don't bring the consistent daily effort, it's not going to happen.

You have to keep the long-term focus while constantly achieving short-term goals. Keep in mind that most people are going to be working a job for 40 years. It's not too much to ask for you to invest 2 - 5 years to build a Multi-Million Dollar MLM Business that produces you serious "Residual Income" month after month, year after year, whether you work or not. Some will get it faster than others. The important thing is that you get it and get free. Don't look back. Stay focused on the "Shortcut" I've provided for you in this book.

You've got to decide right now that you are willing to pay the price. There's "no free rides" in MLM. This is not a "Get Rich

Quick Scheme." However, to me and many others, it is the quickest way for the average person to get rich, but it takes a lot of effort and a lot of work. It's worth every bit of it. When you make it, you won't feel any of the pain it took you to get there. Your lifestyle will blow you and others away.

To make it happen, you're going to have to truly take advantage of everything you've learned in this book. If you want to duplicate yourself quickly, a good way to do so is to have all your team members purchase a copy of this book.

Focus on getting at least 10 other people on your team to get a copy of this book, and all of you start applying the techniques at the same time. Watch what happens!

And by the way, this is **your copy** of the book. You invested in you. Don't give it away to someone else. It won't work for them anyway, because they didn't invest in themselves (a major success principle). I've seen people for years trying to "cheat" their way to success. It's not going to happen. **You have to pay YOUR price**. Success requires from each of us that we pay our own personal price.

I'm confident that through our time together through the pages of this book that you have become stronger. You now have in your possession what every person in the MLM Industry wants... A true Million Dollar MLM Shortcut.

Now, go make your dreams come true!

Be sure to stay plugged in to my website for cutting edge training material. My mission is to help train and inspire1,000 Millionaires. I hope you become the next one.

www.JayNolandMLM.com

My Best,

Jay Noland
Million Dollar MLM Shortcut

CPSIA information can be obtained at www.ICGtesting.com
Printed in the USA
BVOW08s0842151215

430328BV00001B/216/P